# GLUTEN AND GLUTEN FREE COOKING IN PERFECT HARMONY TAKE 2

The One Recipe Solution to Accommodate Everyone

Lucie Cote Contente

Gluten and Gluten Free Cooking in Perfect Harmony Take 2
The One Recipe Solution to Accommodate Everyone
All Rights Reserved.
Copyright © 2018 Lucie Cote Contente
v4.0

The opinions expressed in this manuscript are solely the opinions of the author and do not represent the opinions or thoughts of the publisher. The author has represented and warranted full ownership and/or legal right to publish all the materials in this book.

This book may not be reproduced, transmitted, or stored in whole or in part by any means, including graphic, electronic, or mechanical without the express written consent of the publisher except in the case of brief quotations embodied in critical articles and reviews.

Outskirts Press, Inc.
http://www.outskirtspress.com

ISBN: 978-1-9772-0275-8

Cover Photo © 2018 Lucie Cote Contente. All rights reserved - used with permission.

Outskirts Press and the "OP" logo are trademarks belonging to Outskirts Press, Inc.

PRINTED IN THE UNITED STATES OF AMERICA

# Acknowledgments

I would like to thank my husband for always being there and encouraging me. Gluten free didn't just change my life, it changed for everyone around me. Thank you for wanting to understand my food limitations and helping me on my journey. Thank you to Lynda for taking the time to edit my books and always wanting the best for me. JJ, you are my sunshine.

# Table of Contents

The Journey Continues ..................................................................i
Why a Second Cookbook? ........................................................ iii
Finding the Right Nutritionist ................................................... v
Why Is Adherence Important? .................................................. vi
A Second Food Allergy ............................................................. vii
Food Alternatives ..................................................................... viii
Helpful Conversions ................................................................. ix

### RECIPES

**BREAKFAST** ............................................................................ 3
    Banana Muffins ................................................................. 4
    Pancakes ............................................................................ 5
    Apple Muffins ................................................................... 6
    Pumpkin Bread ................................................................. 7
    Cranberry Orange Breakfast Bars ..................................... 8
    Raspberry Lemon Scone ................................................. 10
    Veggie Omelette .............................................................. 12
    Quiche with Potato Crust ............................................... 13
    Spice Donut with Maple Glaze ....................................... 14
    Parfait .............................................................................. 16
    Banana Pumpkin Muffin ................................................ 17

**LUNCH** ................................................................................ 19
    Canadian Pea Soup ......................................................... 20
    Hot Chicken Sandwich .................................................. 21
    Lentil Soup ..................................................................... 22
    Shrimp Pasta Salad ......................................................... 23
    Ham Salad ...................................................................... 24
    3 Bean Salad ................................................................... 25

Pasta Salad.................................................................26
Creton Meat Spread ...................................................27
Spring Rolls................................................................28
B.L.*E*.T. (Bacon, Lettuce, Egg and Tomato) .............29
Egg Salad ...................................................................30
Mixed Green Salad with Pear......................................31
Soft Tortillas...............................................................32
Italian Wedding Soup.................................................33
Latkes.........................................................................34

## DINNER .................................................................37

Beef Stew ...................................................................38
Canadian Meat Stuffing .............................................39
Spaghetti with Red Clam Sauce..................................40
Baked Fish..................................................................41
Meatballs....................................................................42
Oven Roasted Garlic Rosemary Potatoes ....................43
Shepherd's Pie ............................................................44
Baked Stuffed Shells ...................................................45
Roast Beef...................................................................46
Fricassee .....................................................................47
Chicken Parmesan......................................................48
Shrimp Mozambique..................................................49
Chourico and Peppers.................................................50
Chicken Kiev ..............................................................51
Rosemary Scallops......................................................52
Italian Chicken...........................................................53
Penne with Vegetables ................................................54
Tex Mex Chicken Stew................................................55
Baked Stuffed Peppers ................................................56

**DESSERT** .................................................................................. **59**
    Carrot Cake Cupcakes ............................................................. 60
    Apple Pie Crumble .................................................................. 62
    Oatmeal Raisin Cookies .......................................................... 63
    Lemon Squares ....................................................................... 64
    Portuguese Rice Pudding ....................................................... 65
    Chocolate Chip Cookies ......................................................... 66
    Mocha ...................................................................................... 67
    Crispy Rice Treats ................................................................... 68
    Brownies .................................................................................. 69
    Ricotta Cookies ....................................................................... 70
    Pineapple Upside Down Mini Cakes ..................................... 71
    Thumbprint Cookies ............................................................. 72
    Sugar Cookies ......................................................................... 73
    Coconut Macaroons ............................................................... 74
    Grimace ................................................................................... 75

**POTPOURI** ............................................................................... **77**
    Chicken Gravy ........................................................................ 78
    Coleslaw ................................................................................... 79
    Honey Dijon Salad Dressing ................................................. 80
    Belly Burn Salad Dressing ..................................................... 81
    Italian Salad Dressing ............................................................ 82

**DRINKS** ................................................................................... **85**
    Tropical Passion ...................................................................... 86
    Vodka Cranberry Cocktail ..................................................... 87
    Party Punch ............................................................................ 88
    Cocoa Mo ................................................................................ 89
    Blueberry Mojito .................................................................... 90

# The Journey Continues

My life has changed for the better since my first cookbook was published in 2017. I joined the Association of Rhode Island Authors (ARIA) which opened up a whole new world of meeting new people. I go to book expos and love meeting and talking with people who are at the beginning of their gluten free food journey. I know that when I speak with someone in the same situation, I truly understand how they feel. I just want to help them as much as I can by giving them all the information I have learned. It makes me happy that someone else will have an easier time than I did on their gluten free journey. I have done some presentations and food tastings at local libraries. No matter if someone had a food allergy or not, they enjoyed the food and couldn't tell it was gluten free. I didn't know this was going to be my journey a year ago but I feel blessed to be doing this and I am happy you are on the journey with me.

The feedback on the first cookbook has been wonderful. Here's a few:

"Great book for families that have both Gluten Free and Non-Gluten Free diets. This book gives tasty recipes that can accomodate both diets."

"If you're looking for an easy to follow cookbook with great recipes this is it! This book is both educational and personal from the author, I look forward to trying more recipes."

"Gluten and Gluten Free Cooking in perfect Harmony has converted me to be Gluten Free in most of my recipes!! I am a cook and I love to cook, this book makes it soooo easy to follow and the taste is no different to many of my favorite recipes and new recipes that Lucie has provided. Thank you Lucie for writing a well done book for those who love to cook and who want to cook healthy !!"

"What a great cookbook, easy to make delicious recipes. Pictures were wonderful to see the finished product."

"Many tasty recipes. We have really enjoyed using this book as part of a healthier lifestyle. Even our 10 year old was happy! Highly recommend!"

I posted all the unedited feedback on my cookbook website www.glutenandglutenfreecookinginperfectharmony.com

It has been such a wonderful experience that I decided to write a second cookbook.

# Why a Second Cookbook?

Why not?! No, really, I felt like I had a little more to share with everyone. I live with not being able to eat gluten and most dairy products. It was a process to avoid gluten and to be able to create recipes that I used to like, making them gluten free and delicious. Lately not only have I continued to focus on gluten free, but I also have tried to reincorporate foods that had dairy but make them dairy free. This book has many gluten free recipes, but for the ones with dairy, I have substituted dairy free options. Most people who have one food allergy usually end up with two. I've spoken to many people and 90% have a second allergy. The majority have been gluten and dairy, gluten and egg or gluten and corn. I love that people share with me how they push through their allergies by substituting foods and they can cook some of their favorite foods and not have to go without. I will share this information later on in the book. If I can help one person with a food allergy have an easier time on their journey, then I have accomplished what I set out to do.

I say it all the time that no one thinks about gluten as much as when you are allergic to it. Even at the holidays, most people see a table full of traditional favorites. I see it as an anxiety riddled moment since I know that most foods are not safe for me. I question the ingredients in everything I see. Some people might get offended or hurt that you are questioning their food, but it is important to think only about you and how you will feel tomorrow. In the past, some of the foods were from cans and who knows what the ingredients were? Cross contamination is very likely too. Better safe than sorry is my motto. Yes, food life is not as easy as it was but stressing over food is never something I thought I would do. Oh, the days of just showing up to someone's house and enjoying everything on the table are over but let's find the bright side; I know I don't overeat, and I don't go home feeling like I gained 10 pounds either, LOL.

I originally started sharing anything I knew or learned about on a blog I had. I took the recipes off and wrote my first cookbook Gluten and Gluten Free Cooking in Perfect Harmony. I created a website and Facebook page with the cookbook's title. Although I can't put the brands of the foods I use to cook in my cookbooks you can go to the website to see them. I have a lot of the information on this site so check it out!

We all lead busy lives. What makes my cookbooks different from other gluten free books is that the recipes are made for food diverse families, people with and without gluten free issues and creating one recipe for the whole family with one little tweak, or a "root recipe". Let me explain. The main part of the recipe is like a tree trunk or the part everyone can eat. Then, imagine the roots of the tree, where you separate the main mixture and add the gluten free/non gluten free ingredient to complete the recipe. These recipes were created for people who don't want to cook two meals in a household where not everyone is gluten free. The best part is that the gluten free person gets to eat exactly what the non gluten free person eats.

There are so many times when you leave your house as a gluten free person that you don't feel "normal" when going to various places such as carnivals, festivals, restaurants and even house parties. Why not feel normal at home? I like to cook with basic ingredients that are already in your kitchen. This was the inspiration for my book.

One day I was in a room of women close to my age and I was listening to them talk about all their issues: hot flashes, gaining weight, hormones, skin issues and a bunch more. I realized at that point that I don't have any of those things and I realized that eating gluten and dairy free had some positives to it. I know that it has helped with my blood sugars, my weight, my heartburn is gone, my mood, my skin and my energy level. It's hard to find the bright side of things sometimes, but when given lemons (good thing they are gluten free, lol), it's just easier to make some lemonade.

# Finding the Right Nutritionist

Last fall, I went to see a new nutritionist because I needed to take control of my health. At the end of the summer, I had anxiety and my hair was falling out. I made an appointment to see my physician. I found out I was vitamin deficient from not eating gluten. I had been given new thyroid medicine and one of the side effects was hair loss. My sugar levels were high and I didn't feel good about myself. I made an appointment with a new nutritionist. At the first visit I can only describe that I felt like I was in the middle of a maze and couldn't get out. She ended up being the answer to what I needed at that time. Between getting on the right vitamins to correct the deficiency and changing some eating habits, I started feeling better. I know this sounds strange, but maybe it will help someone who is reading this. I downloaded an app that I inputted all the food I had daily and any exercise I did. The nutritionist said I was eating 1200 calories and that was not enough for me. She also noticed that I was going too long between meals without eating. I upped the calories to 1500 and ate every 3 hours. I started losing weight and my sugar numbers were better. She was very knowledgeable on how to help someone like me who had multiple co morbidities (the presence of two chronic conditions in a person). She explained the pros and cons of food choices. Using natural peanut butter instead of my favorite peanut butter because sometimes your body doesn't process chemicals well. Adding lower sugar jelly instead of the one I used for years but tasted just as good. Being given permission to not feel guilty over eating a healthy snack late at night because it would help my body go less time without eating and it would help lower my morning diabetic sugar levels.

# Why Is Adherence Important?

I'm the type of person who tries to "follow the rules", so when my doctor diagnosed me with Celiac I knew I had to make changes. I tried to read everything I could, but there is a saying in the business world: you don't know what you don't know. I didn't know what I was looking for but I just knew I had to learn about Celiac. Even though I am a few years into this new lifestyle, I still try to understand Celiac and what it entails. Here is some of the information I found about why it's important to adhere to a gluten free diet:

People with Celiac need to know that it is very important not to eat gluten. I know that not everyone has the same level of pain if they eat gluten (mine is severe). I think it is a blessing to "feel" the gluten because if I didn't, I would eat gluten and not be aware of the damage it is doing in my body. But if you eat gluten, it will enflame your intestines and damage your villi. Villi are tiny hair like structures that project inwards from the lining of the small intestine. Although the villi play a role in digestion, they also are essential for the absorption of digested nutrients. This absorption makes vitamins and nutrients available to your blood and lymphatic fluid. If you have Celiac and eat gluten, the villi flatten out and the intestinal lining becomes damaged which decreases the area that can absorb nutrients. This will lead to your risk of malnutrition as well as vitamin and mineral deficiencies. Over time, the effects of Celiac disease increase due to the decreased efficiency of the small intestine and the damage to the villi. Other symptoms may develop such as anemia, fatigue and bone loss. The malabsorption of nutrients puts your body at risk for other conditions such as weight loss or seizures. Flattened villi is typically the result of villi that have eroded away because of constant inflammation. It can take several months to repair damaged intestinal villi, especially entirely flattened villi. Villi damaged or killed will be able to grow back in most cases if the person stops the intake of gluten. The villi will regenerate in a few days.

# A Second Food Allergy

The day the specialist told me I had an allergy to gluten and lactose, I was shocked! As if one food allergy wasn't enough, now dairy products too? I had been avoiding gluten for years because it bothered my stomach but now dairy? When gluten was not an option anymore, I focused my food around dairy. My choices from the food pyramid were becoming slim. At first, I did think it was lactose intolerance but then I tried foods that were lactose free, I quickly realized that I was dairy intolerant. I noticed that unlike gluten which took up to 48 hours for my body to respond, dairy only took a few hours to respond. From that point on, I stopped eating all dairy for one year and focused on the gluten free diet. After a year, I started to try different dairy products to see if I could tolerate any. There were a few that I could incorporate into my life in moderation. The list was minimal, but I was thankful for the few items. I started to talk to people with non-traditional diets to see what I could incorporate into my daily food life. I found "cheese" slices that were not dairy but strangely tasted like the cheese I used to eat. I bought heart healthy butter alternative, which tastes great. One day I put the cheese with the gluten free bread and made what I called a "fake" grilled cheese. Seriously, it was delicious!! This gave me hope. If I could find this "cheese", what else would be out there? I looked up more dairy alternatives and found more foods to incorporate into my food life. It's amazing the foods I now know about and that I never would have tried if this food allergy hadn't happened. I have posted the dairy free alternative products on my website www.glutenandglutenfreecookinginperfectharmony.com if you want to know more.

# Food Alternatives

I have had the privilege of meeting people with different food allergies and they have shared with me what they do to make their foods tasty.

<u>Egg alternative</u>
oil
milk
baking powder

<u>Milk alternative</u>
Almond milk
Soy milk
Coconut creamer

<u>Cornstarch alternative</u>
Arrowroot
Potato starch

All the recipes can use the same amount of regular flour instead of gluten free flour.

All recipes can use the same amount of regular milk instead of almond milk.

Please note I am not a nutritionist, but I have spent years learning from them throughout my journey.

Most of these recipes have either been passed down to me by family or friends or I took one of my own existing recipes and made it gluten free.

I believe you will enjoy these recipes, my family and friends do.

I am also not a professional chef, I just want to make our gluten free life better.

# Helpful Conversions

| Cup | = | Fluid oz | = | Tbsp | = | Tsp | = | Milliliter |
|---|---|---|---|---|---|---|---|---|
| 1 C | | 8 oz | | 16 tbsp | | 48 tsp | | 237 ml |
| 3/4 C | | 6 oz | | 12 tbsp | | 36 tsp | | 177 ml |
| 1/2 C | | 4 oz | | 8 tbsp | | 24 tsp | | 118 ml |
| 1/4 C | | 2 oz | | 4 tbsp | | 12 tsp | | 59 ml |
| 1/8 C | | 1 oz | | 2 tbsp | | 6 tsp | | 30 ml |
| 1/16 C | | 1/2 oz | | 1 tbsp | | 3 tsp | | 15 ml |

| Gallon | = | Quart | = | Pint | = | Cup | = | Ounce | = | Liter |
|---|---|---|---|---|---|---|---|---|---|---|
| 1 | | 4 qt | | 8 pt | | 16 C | | 128 fl oz | | 3.79 L |
| 1/2 | | 2 qt | | 4 pt | | 8 C | | 64 fl oz | | 1.89 L |
| 1/4 | | 1 qt | | 2 pt | | 4 C | | 32 fl oz | | .95 L |
| 1/8 | | 1/2 qt | | 1 pt | | 2 C | | 16 fl oz | | .47 L |
| 1/16 | | 1/4 qt | | 1/2 pt | | 1 C | | 8 fl oz | | .24 L |
| 1/32 | | 1/8 qt | | 1/4 pt | | 1/2 C | | 4 fl oz | | .12 L |

# RECIPES

# BREAKFAST

# Banana Muffins

*I hate throwing away bananas when they are too ripe for us to eat. I love banana muffins and bread, so this is a great way to use those ripe bananas.*

- 1 C Sugar
- 2 eggs
- 4 oz applesauce
- 1 tsp vanilla
- 1 Lemon rind
- 1/4 tsp salt
- 1 tsp baking powder
- 1 tsp baking soda
- 4 ripe bananas

ROOT INGREDIENTS

- 3/4 C gluten free All purpose flour
- 2 C regular All purpose flour

*\*If only making 1 recipe of regular or gluten free muffins, use 2 Cups of either flour.*

In a large bowl mash the bananas. Add sugar, eggs, applesauce, lemon rind and vanilla and mix together. Mix in baking powder, salt and baking soda. Separate mixture, take 1 C mixture put it in a separate bowl (this will be your gluten free mix). Add 3/4 C gluten free flour and stir. Put in muffin pan. In the first bowl add 1 1/2 C regular flour and stir. Put in separate muffin pan. Bake at 375 for 20 minutes.

# Pancakes

*My father gave me 2 recipes when I got engaged to be married over 30 years ago. It's the way he always made me pancakes when I was growing up. Because this recipe has few ingredients, I will separate the gluten and gluten free recipe.*

GLUTEN FREE

- 1 1/2 C gluten free All purpose flour
- 1 egg
- 1/2 tsp baking powder
- 1/3 C milk (almond milk)
- 1/8 C sugar

REGULAR

- 2 C All purpose flour
- 1 egg
- 1/2 tsp baking powder
- 1 1/4 C milk
- 1/4 C sugar

Mix the ingredients in a bowl. Cook in a pan or on a griddle until golden brown. Serve with fruit or maple syrup.

# Apple Muffins

- 1/2 C sugar
- 1/2 C brown sugar
- 4 oz applesauce
- 2 eggs
- 1 tsp vanilla
- 4 medium apples, peeled, cored and chopped
- 1/2 C milk
- 2 tsp baking powder
- 2 tsp cinnamon

ROOT INGREDIENTS

- 1/2 C gluten free All purpose flour
- 1 1/2 C regular All purpose flour

*If only making 1 recipe of regular or gluten free muffins, use 2 Cups of either flour.*

In a large bowl add sugar, applesauce, eggs milk, apples and vanilla and mix together. Mix in baking powder, salt and cinnamon. Separate mixture, take 1/2 C mixture put it in a separate bowl (this will be your gluten free mix). Add 1/2 C gluten free flour and stir. Put in muffin pan. In the first bowl add 1 1/2 C regular flour and stir. Put in separate muffin pan. Bake at 375 for 19 minutes.

# Pumpkin Bread

*I make bread and muffins with this recipe. I put the oatmeal on the gluten free one to not get them mixed up.*

- 1 C sugar
- 3 eggs
- 4 oz applesauce
- 1-15 oz can pumpkin
- 1/4 C vegetable oil
- 1 C maple syrup
- 2 tsp baking soda
- 1 tsp baking powder
- 1/2 tsp salt
- 1 tsp cinnamon
- 1 tsp nutmeg
- 1/2 tsp all spice
- Raisins (optional)
- Xanthan gum (for the gluten free mix)

### ROOT INGREDIENTS
- 1/2 C gluten free All purpose flour
- 1 1/2 C regular All purpose flour

*\*If only making 1 recipe of regular or gluten free bread, use 2 Cups of either flour.*

In a large bowl mix the first 11 ingredients together. Separate mixture, take 2 1/4 C mixture put it in a separate bowl (this will be your gluten free mix). Add 1 C gluten free flour, 1/4 tsp xanthan gum and stir. Put in greased bread pan and sprinkle with oatmeal. In the first bowl add 1 C regular flour and stir. Put in greased bread pan. Bake at 350 for 50 minutes.

# Cranberry Orange Breakfast Bars

- 5 tbsp butter, room temperature
- 4 oz applesauce
- 1 egg
- 1/3 C brown sugar
- 1 tsp vanilla
- 1/2 tsp baking powder
- 1/2 tsp baking soda
- 1/4 tsp salt
- 1/2 tsp cinnamon
- 1/4 tsp pumpkin pie spice
- 1/4 tsp nutmeg
- 1 1/2 C cranberries
- 3/4 C gluten free oats
- 1 tsp orange rind, grated

ROOT INGREDIENTS

- 1/3 C gluten free All purpose flour
- 1/2 C regular All purpose flour

*If only making 1 recipe of regular or gluten free bars, use 1 Cup of either flour.*

In a large bowl mix first 5 ingredients then add all the ingredients except the flour and mix. Separate mixture, take 3/4 C mixture put it in a separate bowl (this will be your gluten free mix). Add 1/3 C gluten free flour. Put in greased pan. In the first bowl add 1/2 C regular flour and stir. Put in greased pan. Bake at 350 for 20 minutes.

## ICING

- 1 C confectioner's sugar
- 1/2 tsp vanilla
- 2 tbsp butter, melted
- Juice of 1 small orange

Mix all together and spread on the bars.

# Raspberry Lemon Scone

- 1/3 C sugar
- Zest of 1 lemon
- 1 tsp vanilla
- 6 tbsp butter, room temperature
- 4 oz applesauce
- 1/3 C milk (I used original unsweetened almond milk)
- 2 eggs
- 1/2 tsp salt
- 1 C raspberries
- 1 1/2 tsp baking powder
- 1/4 tsp xanthan gum

### ROOT INGREDIENTS

- 3/4 C gluten free All purpose flour
- 1 1/2 C regular All purpose flour

*If only making 1 recipe of regular or gluten free scones, use 2 Cups of either flour.*

In a large bowl mix first 8 ingredients then baking powder and raspberries and mix. Separate mixture, take 3/4 C mixture put it in a separate bowl (this will be your gluten free mix). Add 3/4 C gluten free flour and 1/4 tsp xanthan gum and mix. In the first bowl add 1 1/2 C regular flour and stir. Using separate spaces, Pat the dough into a circle about 1 inch thick. Cut circle into 4-6 wedges. Place wedges on a greased cookie sheet. Sprinkle sugar on top. Bake at 350 for 25 minutes.

## ICING

- 1 C confectioner's sugar
- 1/2 tsp vanilla
- 3 tbsp butter, melted
- Juice of 1/2 lemon

Mix all together and drizzle on the scones.

# Veggie Omelette

- 6 eggs
- Pinch of salt and pepper
- Any vegetables you have available, I used
- 1/4 sweet pepper, chopped
- 1/4 onion, chopped
- 1 tomato, cut up
- 1/4 zucchini, cut up
- 1 tsp parsley
- 2 tbsp shredded cheddar cheese

Marinate all the vegetables in 1 tbsp olive oil on stove for 5 minutes. Put aside in a small bowl. Add eggs, salt and pepper to a bowl and whisk together. Spray a pan and add half the egg mixture. Once there is almost no wet eggs on top, flip the omelette over. Using only one half of the omelette, add a tsp worth of cheese, then the vegetables and one more tsp of cheese on top of vegetables. Flip over the other half of the omelette and let cook for 30 seconds. Flip omelette over to the other side for 30 seconds and it's done.

# Quiche with Potato Crust

- 5 eggs
- 3 scallions, cut up
- 4 oz mushrooms, sliced
- 1/2 C milk (I use almond milk)
- 1/3 C cheese (I use shredded cheddar)
- 1 tbsp olive oil
- 1/4 tsp salt
- 1/4 tsp pepper
- 1 tbsp corn starch
- 3 breakfast sausage links, cooked and cut up

CRUST

- 1 1/2 C potatoes, shredded
- 1 small onion, shredded
- 1 egg, beaten

Mix all the quiche ingredients together in a bowl and set aside. In a separate bowl combine the crust ingredients. Flatten evenly in a 9 inch pie plate and bake in the oven at 400 for 20 minutes. Remove from oven and pour the quiche mixture in the crust. Bake with the mixture at 400 for 35 minutes, let cool for 20 minutes.

# Spice Donut with Maple Glaze

*Donut and maple, what more can you ask for. These are very tasty!*

- 1/3 C brown sugar
- 1 C pumpkin puree
- 2 eggs
- 4 oz applesauce
- 1/4 C butter, softened
- 1 1/2 tsp baking powder
- 1 1/2 tsp pumpkin pie spice
- 1/2 tsp salt
- 1/4 tsp baking soda
- 1/2 tsp cinnamon

ROOT INGREDIENTS
- 1/3 C gluten free All purpose flour
- 2/3 C regular All purpose flour

*If only making 1 recipe of regular or gluten free donuts, use 1 Cup of either flour.

In a large bowl mix the first 5 ingredients then add the rest of the ingredients and mix together. Separate mixture, take 1 C of mixture put it in a separate bowl (this will be your gluten free mix). Add 1/3 C gluten free flour. In the first bowl add 2/3 C regular flour and mix together. Spray donut pans. Put mixtures in separate plastic zip lock bag and cut corner of bag. It is easier to squeeze mixture into the donut pan. Bake at 350 for 10 minutes.

While donuts baking, make the glaze.

## GLAZE

- 1 1/2 C confectioner sugar
- 3 tbsp maple syrup
- 1/4 C butter, melted
- 1/2 tsp vanilla

I used a blender to mix all the ingredients. Let donuts cool for 3 minutes and dunk them in the glaze while still warm. Make the gluten free ones first.

# Parfait

*Because I can't have dairy, I used vanilla coconut milk yogurt for mine. Delicious!*

- 5 oz Vanilla yogurt 1/2 C Granola, gluten free
- 1/2 C Blueberries
- 1/2 C Strawberries, sliced

Add 2 tablespoons of yogurt to the bottom of a cup. Add 1/2 C blueberries and on top of that 1/2 C sliced strawberries. Add 2 tablespoons of yogurt and finish it off with 1/2 C of granola.

# Banana Pumpkin Muffin

- 2 tbsp butter
- 4 ripe bananas
- 1 tsp vanilla
- 1/2 C maple syrup
- 1/2 C pumpkin puree
- 1 tsp cinnamon
- 1/4 tsp salt
- 1 tsp baking soda
- 1 tsp baking powder
- 1/4 tsp nutmeg
- 1/4 tsp all spice

### TOPPING

- 2 tbsp butter, softened
- 1/4 C brown sugar
- 1/4 tsp cinnamon
- 1/2 C oatmeal

### ROOT INGREDIENTS

- 3/4 C gluten free All purpose flour
- 2 C regular All purpose flour

*If only making 1 recipe of regular or gluten free muffins, use 2 Cups of either flour.*

In a large bowl mash the bananas. Add all the other ingredients and mix together. Separate mixture, take 1 C mixture put it in a separate bowl (this will be your gluten free mix). Add 1/2 C gluten free flour and stir. Put in muffin pan. In the first bowl add 1 1/4 C regular flour and and stir. Put in separate muffin pan. Add 1 tbsp of topping to each muffin. Bake at 375 for 20 minutes.

# LUNCH

*SOUPS, SALADS AND STUFF*

# Canadian Pea Soup

*I am Canadian and my mother makes the best pea soup. Sharing a family tradition!*

- 2 C dried yellow peas
- 2 quarts plus 1 C cold water
- 6 oz salt pork
- 1 onion, minced
- 1/2 C celery, minced
- 2 carrots, chopped
- 1/4 C parley
- 1 tsp salt
- 1/2 tsp pepper
- 1/2 tsp ground allspice

Soak the peas overnight. Next day, drain the peas and put in a pot with new water to cover peas. Boil the peas for 10 minutes then drain. Place the peas in a large pot, add cold 2 quarts plus 1 C cold water, salt pork, onion, celery, carrots, allspice, parsley, salt and pepper. Bring to a boil and lower heat and simmer, covered for 3 hours. After 2 hours of cooking, remove salt pork. Separate meat from fat off salt pork. Put the salt pork meat back in the soup.

# Hot Chicken Sandwich

*My uncle used to have a restaurant in Canada and this was on the menu. When we visited him this was our favorite dish to order. Another meal that was a staple in my house growing up. My children love it now. It is a chicken sandwich with brown gravy, french fries and vegetables.*

- 2 slices of Bread, gluten free
- 1 package brown gravy, gluten free
- French fries-recipe in book 1
- 1 C cooked chicken—I use rotisserie
- 1 C cooked vegetable—I use peas

Cook the french fries. Cook or warm up the vegetables. Cook the gluten free brown gravy. On a plate add the chicken to a slice of bread. Pour gravy on top of the chicken. Add the other slice of bread. Add the french fries to the plate. Pour gravy over the bread and french fries. Add the vegetable on top of bread. Enjoy!!

# Lentil Soup

*A few years ago we went out with friends on New Year's eve to an Italian restaurant in the city. They were serving a seven course meal. The soup that night was lentil. The waitress told us when you eat lentil soup on New Year's it gives you good luck in the year to come. I believed her and have had it ever since.*

- 2 C dry lentils, rinsed
- 8 C vegetable broth, gluten free
- 2 medium potatoes, peeled and cubed
- 1 onion, chopped
- 1 celery stalk, chopped
- 1 carrot, diced
- 1 tsp parsley
- 1 tsp oregano
- 1 tsp basil
- 1 bay leaf
- 1 tsp salt
- 1/2 tsp pepper
- 2 cloves garlic minced
- 2 tsp olive oil
- 1 14.5 can chopped tomatoes
- 1 tsp sugar
- 1/4 tsp crushed red peppers
- 2 tbsp olive oil

In a large pot, add olive and marinate onion, celery, carrot and garlic for 2 minutes. Add broth, oregano, basil, parsley, salt, pepper, bay leaf, potatoes, tomatoes, sugar, crushed red pepper and lentils. Bring to a boil, reduce heat and cook for 30 minutes.

# Shrimp Pasta Salad

- 12 oz bow tie pasta, gluten free
- 6 hard boiled eggs, cut up
- 30 green olives sliced
- 4 oz can tiny shrimps, drained
- Salt and pepper to taste
- 1/2 tsp parsley
- 1/2 tsp onion powder
- 1/2 tsp garlic powder
- 1 tbsp olive oil
- 3 tbsp mayonaise
- Paprika

Cook the pasta according to directions on package adding 1 extra minute. Drain water and let pasta cool then add to a large bowl. Add the olive oil, parsley, onion powder, garlic powder, salt and pepper and mix. Add the eggs, olives, shrimps and mayonnaise and mix. Sprinkle the top with parsley and paprika. Let cool for 1 hour in the refrigerator.

# Ham Salad

*Ever have left over ham and not know what to make with it? When my mother makes a ham, you know the next day there will be ham salad and pea soup. I wanted to put it in this cookbook to share the easy recipe with you all.*

- 5 lbs cooked ham, remove fat
- 1 large onion
- 3 tbsp mayonnaise

Grind the ham and the onion together. Add the mayonnaise and refrigerate. That's it! See, so easy. Enjoy!

# 3 Bean Salad

*I make this cold salad a lot during the summer. So easy to make. My husband eats it as a meal. I like it as a side dish.*

- 15 oz can cut green beans, drained
- 15 oz can cannellini beans, drained and rinsed
- 15 oz can red kidney beans, drained and rinsed
- 1/2 Vidalia onion, cut up
- 1/4 C olive oil
- 1 tbsp honey
- 1/2 C apple cider vinegar
- 1/4 tsp garlic powder
- 1/4 tsp salt and pepper

In a large bowl, add the beans and onion. In a smaller bowl add olive oil, honey, vinegar, garlic powder, salt and pepper and whisk together. Add the dressing to the large bowl and mix all together.

# Pasta Salad

- 8 oz box of pasta, gluten free
- 1/2 green pepper, cut up
- 1 carrot, shredded
- 1/2 sweet onion, cut up
- 1 tomato, cut up
- 1 cucumber, cut up
- 1 tsp parsley
- 1/2 tsp garlic powder
- 1/2 tsp salt
- 1/4 tsp pepper
- 2 tbsp olive oil
- Italian dressing, gluten free

Cook the pasta according to the box directions. Once done, strain the water and put the pasta in a bowl to cool. Once cooled, add olive oil, parsley, garlic powder, salt and pepper and mix with a spoon. Add all the vegetables and Italian dressing and mix all together. Put in the refrigerator for 1 hour and serve.

# Creton Meat Spread (Pronounced Like Cra-ton)

*This is a Canadian meat spread. I eat it as a sandwich for lunch or on toast in the morning. Some add condiments. All taste delicious!*

- 4 lbs pork roast with fat
- 1 large onion
- Salt and pepper to taste

Put the pork roast in a large pot, fill 1/4 of pan with water. Bake in the oven for 3 hours at 350. Remove pork roast from pot and remove the bones and fat. Grind the meat with the onion. Put ground meat and onion back in the broth in the pot. Cook on stove, add salt and pepper to taste. Bring to a boil, reduce heat and continue to cook until most of the broth dissolves, approximately 30 minutes. Let cool and put in containers. Keep in refrigerator. My mother freezes some. The spread lasts up to 6 months in the freezer.

# Spring Rolls

- Spring roll rice wrapper
- 2 carrots, shredded
- 3 green onions, sliced
- 1 garlic clove, minced
- Pinch of salt and pepper
- 1/2 tsp parsley
- 10 shrimps, peeled and deveined
- 2 oz rice sticks (noodles), cooked
- 2 tbsp olive oil

In a pan, marinate carrots, green onions and garlic in 1 tbsp olive oil for 5 minutes, add salt, pepper and parsley. Remove from pan and put in a bowl. Using the same pan, add 1 tbsp olive oil and cook the shrimps until pink. While the shrimps are cooking, bring water to a boil in a small pot and add the 2 oz of rice noodles and cook for 5 minutes. Once the shrimps are done, remove from pan and put in a dish. Cut the shrimps lengthwise. Once the rice noodles are done, drain water out and rinse with cold water. Line up your ingredients like an assembly line….shrimps, vegetables, rice noodles. Get a large bowl out and fill with cold water. Put 1 spring roll rice wrapper in the water. It will take 15-20 seconds for it to get soft. Gently remove from water and put it in a big plate. Take 1 tbsp of vegetables and put in the middle of the wrap, add a few shrimps and some rice noodles. Fold the sides of the wrap in and roll the rest of the wrapper. Place on a dish. Continue with the other wrappers until you run out of ingredients. I eat them just like that, no cooking or frying.

# B.L.*E*.T.
# (Bacon, Lettuce, Egg and Tomato)

*When my kids were little I decided to add eggs to their BLT's. They loved it and that is the only way I make it now.*

- 1 package bacon cooked
- Lettuce
- 1 tomatoes, sliced
- 1 egg, cooked over easy
- Mayonnaise
- 2 slices bread toasted, gluten free

Put the bacon in the oven for 20 minutes at 450. In a pan, cook the egg, over easy breaking and cooking the yolk. Toast the bread. Once all ingredients are ready, put the sandwich together. Add mayonnaise to the inside of both slices of bread. Add tomatoes to one slice and lettuce to the other. Layer the bacon on the lettuce and the egg on the tomatoes. Put the 2 slices together and cut B.L.E.T. in half and enjoy!

# Egg Salad

*I use the same recipe for egg salad and deviled eggs.*

- 6 eggs
- 1 1/2 tsp onion powder
- 1 tbsp mayonnaise

Put the eggs in a pot of water and boil for 15 minutes. Once done, drain water and fill with cold water. Remove the shells while still warm, it's easier. Put eggs in a bowl. Mash eggs with a potato masher or a fork until all are tiny pieces. Let cool for 15 minutes. Once cooled, add the onion powder and mayonnaise and mix. Put in the refrigerator for 30 minutes in a covered container. Serve cold.

# Mixed Green Salad with Pear

*My friend Kim is always asked to bring this delicious salad that she makes.*

- 1 bag field greens
- 1/2 red onion, sliced
- 1 red pear, sliced
- 3/4 container goat cheese
- Dried cranberries
- Chopped walnuts

Mix all together in a bowl and serve with balsamic vinaigrette.

# Soft Tortillas

*These were fun to make and so tasty. I got full after 1 taco so I took one of the other tortilla's and added powdered sugar to it, oh so good! For the taco I added cooked hamburger, refried beans, lettuce, tomato, Mexican 4 cheese and salsa. It was so filling. For dessert I took a soft tortilla and added confectioner's sugar. So delicious! My husband and son love these and they know they are gluten free!*

- 1 C All purpose flour, gluten free
- 1/2 C tapioca flour
- 1 tsp xanthan gum
- 1/2 tsp baking powder
- 1 tsp corn starch
- 1 tsp sugar
- 1/4 tsp salt
- 3/4 C warm water
- Olive oil

Mix the first 7 ingredients together. Add the warm water slowly to the dry ingredients and mix, I used my hands. Knead the dough until fully mixed. Separate dough into 7 even sizes and roll to as thin as possible. I used a bowl to cut the dough to make the tortilla. Heat up 1 tsp olive oil in a pan and add the tortilla. Cook for 1 minute then flip to the other side for 1 minute. Do the same process for the other tortillas.

# Italian Wedding Soup

- 1 onion, chopped
- 2 cloves garlic, minced
- 32 oz chicken broth, gluten free
- 1 tsp parsley
- 1 tsp basil
- 1/2 tsp oregano
- 1/2 tsp salt
- 1/4 tsp pepper
- Meatballs-use recipe on page 42
- 2 C spinach, chopped
- 1 tbsp olive oil
- 2 C water
- 1/2 C pasta, gluten free

In a large pot, heat olive oil and add onions and garlic and marinate for 3 minutes. Add broth, parsley, basil, oregano, salt, pepper, water and meatballs. Bring to a boil for 10 minutes. Reduce heat, add spinach and pasta and cook for 10 minutes

# Latkes

- 1 1/2 lbs russet potatoes, shredded
- 1 large onion, shredded
- 2 eggs, separated
- 1/4 C matzo meal, gluten free
- 1 tbsp salt
- 1/2 tsp pepper
- Vegetable oil

Squeeze the liquid out of the shredded potatoes into a bowl and put aside. Put the squeezed potatoes into a different bowl and add 2 egg yolks (put the egg whites in a separate bowl), onions, matzo meal, salt and pepper and mix together. Whisk the egg whites until small peaks form. In the bowl with the liquid, empty the water on top and keep the potato starch that is at the bottom. Add starch to the potatoes and mix together. Gently mix in the egg whites. Heat a thin layer of vegetable oil in a pan. Scoop a tablespoon of potatoes into the oil. Cook until golden brown.

# DINNER

# Beef Stew

- 1/2 pound stew meat
- 4 potatoes, peeled and cut
- 1 carrot, peeled and sliced
- 1 medium onion, chopped
- 1 celery, chopped
- 32 oz beef broth, gluten free
- 1 C chicken broth, gluten free
- 1/2 tsp granulated bouillon
- 1-16 oz can cut up tomatoes (optional)
- 1 tbsp corn starch
- 8 oz water
- 2 tbsp butter

In a large pot melt butter and add stew meat. Stir for 1 minute to brown the meat. Add the onions, continue to stir meat and onions for 1 minute. Add all the ingredients except corn starch and water. Bring to a boil, reduce to medium heat for 20 minutes. In a bowl mix corn starch and 3/4 C water. Increase heat so stew is boiling again, slowly add the corn starch/water mixture while mixing the stew with a spoon. Let boil 1 minute. Turn stove off and let stew sit 10 minutes.

# Canadian Meat Stuffing

- 1 1/2 lbs of hamburger
- 5 potatoes
- 4 slices bread, gluten free
- Turkey heart
- Turkey liver
- 1 big onion
- 1 tsp salt
- 1/4 tsp pepper
- 2 tbsp bell's seasoning blend
- 2 C water

Grind hamburger, potatoes, bread, onion, turkey heart and liver. Put the ground mix in a large pan and add salt, pepper, bell's seasoning blend and 2 C water. Bring to a boil and lower heat, cover and cook for 20 minutes.

# Spaghetti with Red Clam Sauce

*This is one of those recipes that is easy to make, tastes delicious but somehow tastes even better the next day-if you are lucky enough to have left overs.*

- 28 oz San Marzano crushed tomatoes
- 6.5 oz chopped clams
- 8 oz clam juice
- 1 tbsp olive oil
- 4 cloves garlic, minced
- 1/2 tsp salt
- 1/2 tsp pepper
- 1 tsp oregano
- 2 tbsp butter
- 1/2 C white wine
- 1 C pasta water
- 1 box spaghetti, gluten free

Cook spaghetti according to direction.

Heat olive oil in a pan on medium and add garlic for 1 minute. Add tomatoes, oregano, salt, pepper, clams, clam juice, wine and pasta water and bring to a boil for 4 minutes. Add butter, once melted add spaghetti to sauce.

# Baked Fish

*I had been looking for a tasty baked fish recipe and my friend Robin shared with me how she makes hers. Delicious!*

- 2 lbs cod fish
- Tomato slices
- 1/2 C white wine
- 2 tsp melted butter
- 1 tsp parsley
- 1/2 tsp salt
- 1/2 tsp pepper
- 1/2 tsp crushed red peppers
- Juice of 1 lemon

Line the bottom of a large casserole dish with sliced tomatoes. Layer a piece of fish over the tomatoes. On top of the fish, pour the wine, lemon juice and butter. Sprinkle parsley, salt, pepper and crushed peppers over the fish. Cover with foil and bake at 400 for 30 minutes.

# Meatballs

*My sister told me one of her neighbors makes the best Italian meatballs. Of course I had to try this recipe to see if she was right. I made them gluten free and my sister was right, they are delicious!*

- 1 lb Hamburger
- 1/4 lb ground veal
- 1 egg
- 1/4 C + 2 tbsp Italian bread crumbs, gluten free
- 1 small onion-shredded
- 1/8 C warm water
- 1/2 tsp salt
- 1/4 tsp pepper

In a large bowl mix the hamburger and veal. Mix in the egg, bread crumbs and onion. Lastly, add the warm water. Roll in 2 inch round meatballs. Bake at 350 for 20-25 minutes, turning them 1 time halfway through. Serve them with my pasta sauce from my first cookbook.

# Oven Roasted Garlic Rosemary Potatoes

*Some members of my family love potatoes. I try to be creative and find different ways to cook them. This recipe was very tasty.*

- 6 medium potatoes, peeled and sliced
- 1/8 C Olive oil
- 1 tsp garlic powder
- 1 1/2 tsp rosemary

In a large bowl mix up all the ingredients. Spread out the potato slices on a sprayed cookie sheet. Bake at 400 for 30 minutes, turning them over half after 15 minutes.

# Shepherd's Pie

*I used unsweetened original almond milk for the mashed potatoes*

- 6 medium potatoes, peeled and cut up
- 1 14 oz can creamed corn
- 1 14 oz can corn kernels
- 1 lb hamburger
- 3 tbsp butter (I used smart balance)
- 1/2 C milk
- 1/2 tsp salt

Boil the potatoes for 20 minutes. While potatoes are boiling, in a pan cook and mash the hamburger until completely done. Move the cooked hamburger to a bowl. On top of the hamburger pour the creamed corn and the corn kernels. Once the potatoes are done, strain out the water. Add 3 tbsp butter, salt and 1/2 C of milk to the potatoes and mix until creamy, not lumpy. Add the mashed potatoes on top of the corn and spread around to cover the corn.

# Baked Stuffed Shells

- 1 lb hamburger
- 1/2 tsp salt
- 1/4 tsp pepper
- 8 oz ricotta cheese
- 2 3/4 C pasta sauce-found in book 1
- 1 C shredded mozzarella cheese
- Large pasta shells, gluten free

Cook large pasta shells according to directions on package. In a large pan cook and mash the hamburger until no more red meat. Move the cooked hamburger to a large bowl and let cool for 10 minutes. Add 8 oz ricotta cheese, 1 C pasta sauce and 3/4 C mozzarella cheese and mix.

Once shells are done, rinse with cold water. Using a large casserole dish, cover bottom of dish with 1 C pasta sauce. Fill the shells with the meat mixture and place in casserole dish. Once all filled, spread 3/4 C pasta sauce over the shells. Lastly sprinkle 1/2 C mozzarella cheese over the shells. Bake at 350 for 25 minutes, uncovered.

# Roast Beef

*This can be made with any beef-hide of round roast, top round roast, bottom round roast*

- 5 lbs roast
- 4 garlic cloves, sliced
- 1 large onion, chopped
- 1 stick of butter

### GRAVY

- 1 C cornstarch
- 2 C water
- Salt and pepper to taste

In a pot, melt the butter and add the garlic and onions and marinate until butter browns. Put the roast in the pot and brown the sides. Add water to cover 3/4 of the roast. Bake at 400, covered for 2 hours. Once done, remove the meat from the broth.

### GRAVY

Put the pot on the stove and turn heat to high. Bring to a boil. In a container whisk the cornstarch and water together. Add the cornstarch mixture to the boiling broth. Add salt and pepper to taste. Let boil 2 minutes for gravy to thicken. Strain the gravy.

*Save the leftover meat and gravy for the Fricassee meal tomorrow.

# Fricassee

*My family calls it chiar (pronounced like she-ow). My mom always makes this the day after a roast beef meal. Everyone loves it!*

- Leftover roast beef, cut up
- Leftover gravy
- 1 onion, chopped
- 6 large potatoes, peeled and cubed
- Salt and pepper to taste

Heat the leftover gravy in a pot on medium, whisking the lumps out until smooth. Add cut up roast, onion, salt, pepper and put in the oven and bake at 400 for 2 hours covered.

DINNER | 47

# Chicken Parmesan

- 1 1/2 lb boneless chicken breast, thin cut
- 1 C Italian bread crumbs, gluten free
- 2 eggs
- 1/2 C milk
- Salt
- Pepper
- Pasta sauce
- Mozzarella cheese, shredded
- Olive oil

In a bowl, add 2 eggs and milk and whisk together. In a plate add the bread crumbs. In a pan, heat up 3 tablespoons of olive oil. Dredge each cutlet in the egg mixture and then in the bread crumbs. Put the pieces of cutlets in the olive oil. For thin pieces cook 3 minutes on each side. Remove and put on a cookie sheet. Once all are done, add sauce on top of the cutlet and mozzarella cheese. Bake in the oven at 450 until cheese is melted.

# Shrimp Mozambique

*My friend Suzanne gave me this recipe. Best Shrimp Mozambique I've ever tried.*

- 3 lbs shrimps, peeled and deveined
- 1 stick of butter
- 8 cloves of garlic, chopped
- 1 tbsp salt
- 2 tsp con azafran seasoning
- 1 tsp hot chopped peppers (in a jar)
- 2 C port white wine
- 2 tbsp parsley, chopped
- 1 dash cayenne pepper
- 1 lemon

In a pan, melt butter and marinate garlic for 3 minutes. Add shrimps and cook until barely pink. Once shrimps are turning pink, remove them all from heat with spoon and set aside in a bowl. To the pan add salt, con azafrin seasoning, chopped peppers, cayenne pepper and wine. Simmer for 2 minutes. Add the shrimps back to the pan and cook for 2-3 minutes. When 1 minute is left, add the parsley and juice of 1 lemon.

# Chourico and Peppers

I got this recipe from a coworker 30 years ago. I have been making it ever since. So easy and tasty.

- 2 peppers, sliced
- 2 medium onions, sliced
- 2 chourico sausage, skin off, sliced
- 2 tbsp olive oil
- 2 C traditional pasta sauce

In a large pot, heat up olive oil and add the chourico. Cook for 3 minutes and add the peppers, onions and sauce. Bring to a boil and reduce to low. Cover pot and cook for 30 minutes, stirring occasionally.

# Chicken Kiev

- 1 lb chicken breasts, cut thin

**WET MIXTURE**
- 2 eggs
- 1/4 C milk

**DRY MIXTURE**
- 1 tsp parsley
- 1/2 tsp garlic powder
- 1/2 tsp oregano
- 1/2 tsp basil
- 1/2 C bread crumbs, gluten free
- 1/4 tsp salt and pepper
- 1/4 C All purpose flour, gluten free

**BUTTER MIXTURE**
- 1/4 C butter, room temperature
- 1 tsp parsley
- 1/2 tsp oregano
- Juice from 1/2 lemon
- 2 oz Monterey jack cheese-optional

Spread the butter mixture on one side of the chicken. Roll the chicken and put a toothpick through it to hold the roll. Dip chicken in the wet mixture and then in the dry mixture. In a pan, heat olive oil and cook the rolled chickens, turn until all sides are light brown. Once all sides have cooked, remove from heat and remove toothpicks

# Rosemary Scallops

- 1 lb scallops
- 1 tsp garlic powder
- 2 tsp fresh rosemary
- 1/2 tsp salt
- 1/2 tsp pepper
- 2 tbsp butter

In a bowl add the scallops and the seasonings. Mix them so they scallops have all the seasonings on them. In a hot pan, melt the butter and add the scallops. Cook the scallops for 2 minutes on each side. Remove from heat.

# Italian Chicken

*This is easy and quick and a family favorite.*

- 1 lb boneless chicken breast
- 8 oz Italian dressing, gluten free

Marinate the chicken in the Italian dressing at least 4 hours. Cook either on the grill or the stove 2-3 minutes on each side depending on the thickness.

# Penne with Vegetables

- 12 oz pasta, gluten free
- 2 C chicken broth, gluten free
- 3/4 C peppers, chopped
- 1 head broccoli, chopped
- 1/4 Vidalia onion
- 4 cloves garlic, chopped
- 1 small bunch of green onions, sliced
- 3 carrots, diced
- 4 mushrooms, sliced
- 1/4 tsp crushed red peppers
- Salt/pepper to taste
- 1 tsp parsley
- 14 oz cut tomatoes
- Juice of 1 lemon
- 1 C pasta water
- 2 tbsp olive oil

Cook the pasta according to directions on box. Heat the olive oil up in a large pan and add peppers, broccoli, onion, garlic, green onions, carrots and mushrooms for 8 minutes. Add chicken broth, salt, pepper, parsley, tomatoes, lemon and pasta water and mix together. After pasta is cooked and strained, add to pan and mix all together. Bring to a boil, reduce heat and let cook until broth is almost gone. Remove from heat.

# Tex Mex Chicken Stew

- 2 C rice, cooked
- 1 tbsp olive oil
- 1 small onion, chopped
- 1/2 C peppers, chopped
- 2 C chicken broth, gluten free
- 1 lb chicken, cooked, I use rotisserie chicken
- 1 tsp chili powder
- 1/2 tsp cumin
- Salt/pepper to taste
- 1/2 tsp crushed red peppers
- 1 C salsa, gluten free
- 15 oz can corn, drained
- Juice from 1 lime

In a pot, cook rice to directions on package. In a separate large pot, marinate the onion and peppers in 1 tbsp olive oil for 8 minutes. Add chicken broth, cooked chicken, chili powder, cumin, salt, pepper, crushed red peppers, salsa, corn and cooked rice. Bring to a boil and reduce heat, cover and cook for 15 minutes till broth almost gone. Remove from heat and squeeze lime juice over stew and mix.

# Baked Stuffed Peppers

- 1 1/2 C cooked rice
- 1 lb hamburger
- 1 Carrot, chopped
- 1 celery rib, chopped
- 1 small onion, shredded
- 3 garlic cloves, chopped
- 14 oz cut up tomatoes
- 1/2 tsp basil
- 1/2 tsp oregano
- 1/2 tsp parsley
- Salt/pepper to taste
- 4 peppers, cut in half lengthwise and seeded
- 1/4 C water

In a pot, cook the rice according to the directions on box. In a pan, cook the hamburger and once done move to a bowl. To the same pan, add olive oil and marinate carrot, celery, onion and garlic for 8 minutes and then add to the bowl. Add the cooked rice to the bowl. Add the basil, oregano, parsley and salt an pepper. Mix all the ingredients in the bowl. Add 1/4 C to bottom of 11x13 casserole dish. Place the pepper halves in the dish and fill with the mixture. Add the cut tomatoes on top of the mixture. Cover with foil and bake at 350 for 30 minutes.

# DESSERT

# Carrot Cake Cupcakes

- 3/4 C sugar
- 8 oz applesauce
- 3/4 C brown sugar
- 3 eggs
- 1 tsp vanilla
- 2 tsp baking powder
- 2 tsp cinnamon
- 1 tsp baking soda
- 3/4 tsp salt
- 1/2 tsp nutmeg
- 2 C grated carrots
- 1 C raisins

### ROOT INGREDIENTS

- 3/4 C gluten free All purpose flour
- 1 1/4 C regular All purpose flour

*If only making 1 recipe of regular or gluten free cupcakes or muffins, use 2 Cups of either flour.*

Mix sugar, applesauce, brown sugar, 3 eggs and vanilla. Add baking powder, cinnamon, baking soda, salt, nutmeg and carrots. Separate mixture, take 1 1/2 C of mixture put it in a separate bowl (this will be your gluten free mix). Add 3/4 C gluten free flour and 1/4 C raisins. Mix well and add to cupcake cups. In the original bowl add 1 1/4 C regular flour and 1/2 C raisins. Mix well and add mixture to cupcake cups. Can also bake cake. Bake at 350 for 18 min for muffins and 30 minutes for cake.

**ICING**

- 8 oz cream cheese
- 1/4 C butter softened
- 1/2 tsp vanilla
- 1 Cup confectioner sugar

Using a mixer, mix until all blended. Once cupcakes/cake cools, add icing.

# Apple Pie Crumble

### FILLING

- 8 medium apples, peeled, cored and sliced thin
- 2/3 C sugar
- 1/2 tsp nutmeg
- 1/2 tsp all spice
- 1 tsp cinnamon
- 1 tbsp corn starch
- 1/2 C raisins
- 1/2 C orange juice

### CRUMBLE INGREDIENTS

- 2 C oatmeal, gluten free-in blender
- 1 C oatmeal, gluten free
- 6 tbsp butter softened
- 1/3 C brown sugar

In a bowl, add all the filling ingredients, except orange juice, and mix to coat the apples. Let sit. In another bowl add all the crumble ingredients and mix together.

In an 11x13 casserole dish, add the apple filling and pour the orange juice on top. Add the crumble mixture on top of apples and bake at 350 for 45 minutes.

# Oatmeal Raisin Cookies

- 3/4 C brown sugar
- 1/4 C sugar
- 4 oz applesauce
- 4 tbsp butter, room temperature
- 2 eggs
- 1 tbsp milk
- 1 tsp vanilla
- 1 tsp cinnamon
- 1 tsp baking soda
- 2 tsp baking powder
- 1/4 tsp salt
- 1 1/4 C gluten free oatmeal

ROOT INGREDIENTS

- 1/3 C gluten free All purpose flour
- 1 C regular All purpose flour

*If only making 1 recipe of regular or gluten free cookies, use 1 3/4 Cups of either flour.*

In a large bowl add sugars, eggs, applesauce, butter, milk and vanilla and mix together. Mix in cinnamon, baking powder, salt, baking soda and oatmeal. Separate mixture, take 1/2 C + 1tbsp mixture put it in a separate bowl (this will be your gluten free mix). Add 1/3 C gluten free flour and 1/4 C raisins and stir. In the first bowl add 1 C regular flour and 1/2 C raisins and stir. Bake at 375 for 8 minutes.

*Bake the gluten free cookies first on the cookie sheets and then the regular one to not cross contaminate.*

# Lemon Squares

- 3/4 C All purpose flour, gluten free
- 1/4 C tapioca flour
- 8 tbsp butter, room temperature
- 1/4 C powdered sugar
- 2 eggs
- 1/2 tsp baking powder
- 1 C sugar
- 2 1/2 tbsp lemon juice
- 1 tbsp powdered sugar

In a bowl, mix flours with 1/4 C powdered sugar and butter. Grease an 8x8 pan. Pat mixture evenly into bottom of pan. Bake for 20 minutes at 350. Five minutes before crust is done, make the filling. In a bowl mix eggs, baking powder, sugar and lemon juice. Once crust is removed from oven, pour mixture over crust and bake again for 20 minutes. Let stand till cool, 2 hours. Sprinkle 1 tablespoon powdered sugar over top. Cut into squares to serve.

# Portuguese Rice Pudding

*I use original unsweetened almond milk*

- 4 C milk
- 1 stick butter, 8 tbsp
- 1 C sugar
- 1 C rice
- 3.4 oz French vanilla instant pudding mix, gluten free
- cinnamon

Combine the first four ingredients in a pot and bring to a boil. Reduce the heat to low and cover for 35 minutes until the rice is cooked but there is still liquid. Remove from the heat and stir in the French vanilla pudding. Pour into a 9x11 casserole dish. Let cool on counter for 1 hour. Cover and continue to cool in refrigerator. Right before serving, sprinkle cinnamon on top.

# Chocolate Chip Cookies

*When I make the cookies both gluten free and regular, I use dairy and gluten free chocolate chips for the gluten free cookies and the regular chocolate chips for the regular cookies.*

- 3/4 C sugar
- 3/4 C brown sugar
- 4 oz applesauce
- 6 tbsp butter, room temperature
- 1 tsp vanilla
- 2 eggs
- 1/2 tsp salt
- 1 tsp baking soda
- 1 tsp baking powder
- 1 C Chocolate chips

ROOT INGREDIENTS
- 1/2 C gluten free All purpose flour
- 1 1/2 C regular All purpose flour

*If only making 1 recipe of regular or gluten free cookies, use 2 Cups of either flour.*

Mix first 6 ingredients for 1 minute. Add remaining ingredients and mix with a spoon. Separate mixture, take 3/4 C mixture put it in a separate bowl (this will be your gluten free mix). Add 1/3 C gluten free flour and 1/3 C chocolate chips. In the first bowl add 1 1/4 C regular flour and 3/4 C chocolate chips. Bake at 350 for 7 minutes.

*Bake the gluten free cookies first on the cookie sheets and then the regular ones to not cross contaminate.*

# Mocha

*This recipe originated in France and has been handed down in my mother's family. My grandmother used to make these for her large family gatherings during the holiday season. My mother had 11 siblings, so this is a great recipe for large groups.*

- 1 package yellow cake mix, gluten free
- Cook 3 days prior and cut up in small pieces, cover lightly with foil
- 2 lbs salted peanuts, ground in food processor

### FROSTING

- 8 tbsp butter, room temperature
- 1 tsp vanilla
- 2 C powdered sugar
- 1/2 C milk

Using blender, mix until consistency of whole milk-if need to thicken, add more powdered sugar.

Take a piece of cake, roll it in the frosting and then roll it in the ground peanuts. Put them on cookie sheets to dry. Store them in the refrigerator.

# Crispy Rice Treats

- 10 oz brown rice crisps
- 15 oz marshmallows
- 7 tbsp butter

First use the butter to grease a 13x9 casserole dish then:

In a large pot melt the butter over medium heat. Add marshmallows and let them melt, stirring frequently. I use a hard spatula, easy to grab and mix. Once marshmallows fully melted, remove from heat and add rice crisps. Mix completely and pour into the casserole dish and press down with spatula. Let cool on counter 30 minutes. Cover and finish cooling in refrigerator for 30 minutes. Cut into squares and enjoy.

# Brownies

*For the gluten free brownies I used the dairy and gluten free chocolate chips.*

- 1 C sugar
- 1 C brown sugar
- 3/4 C unsweetened cocoa powder
- 1/2 C cornstarch
- 2 eggs
- 5 tbsp butter, room temperature
- 4 oz applesauce
- 1 tsp baking soda
- 3/4 C Chocolate chips

### ROOT INGREDIENTS

- 1/4 C gluten free All purpose flour
- 1/2 C regular All purpose flour

*\*If only making 1 recipe of regular or gluten free brownies, use 3/4 Cup of either flour.*

Mix first 8 ingredients together. Separate mixture, take 1 C mixture put it in a separate bowl (this will be your gluten free mix). Add 1/4 C gluten free flour and 1/4 C chocolate chips and pour in greased pan. In the first bowl add 1/2 C regular flour and 1/2 C chocolate chips and pour in greased pan. Sprinkle tops of brownie batter with chocolate chips. Bake at 375 for 30 minutes.

# Ricotta Cookies

- 1 C sugar
- 4 oz butter, melted
- 8 oz ricotta
- 1 egg
- 1 tsp vanilla
- 1/4 tsp salt
- 1/2 tsp baking powder
- 1/2 baking soda
- Orange rind
- Xanthan gum (for the gluten free mix)

### ROOT INGREDIENTS

- 1/2 C gluten free All purpose flour
- 2 1/2 C regular All purpose flour

*If only making 1 recipe of regular or gluten free cookies, use 3 Cups of either flour.*

Mix first 5 ingredients then add all the ingredients except the flour and mix together. Separate mixture, take 1 C mixture put it in a separate bowl (this will be your gluten free mix). Add 1/2 C gluten free flour and 1/2 tsp xanthan gum and mix. Drop a tsp worth of dough on cookie sheet. In the first bowl add 2 1/2 C regular flour and mix. Drop a tsp worth of dough on cookie sheet. Bake at 350 for 10 minutes.

### FROSTING

- 1 C powdered sugar
- 2 tbsp butter
- 2 tbsp milk
- 1/2 tsp vanilla

Whisk together, once cooled, drop over cookies and add sprinkles.

# Pineapple Upside Down Mini Cakes

### CAKE

- 2/3 C sugar
- 2 eggs
- 4 tbsp pineapple juice (get from can of crushed pineapple)
- 1 tsp baking powder
- 1/4 tsp salt

### SUGAR MIX

- 1/4 C butter melted
- 3/4 C brown sugar
- 20 oz can crushed pineapple
- cherries

### ROOT INGREDIENTS

- 1/4 C gluten free All purpose flour
- 1/2 C regular All purpose flour

*If only making 1 recipe of regular or gluten free cakes, use 3/4 Cup of either flour.*

In a large bowl mix the 5 cake ingredients together. Separate mixture, take 1/3 C mixture put it in a separate bowl (this will be your gluten free mix). Add 1/4 C gluten free flour and mix. In the first bowl add 1/2 C regular flour and mix. Spray muffin tins. In each section add 1 tbsp crushed pineapples, 1 tsp sugar mix, 1 tbsp cake mix and a cherry on top. Bake at 350 for 12 minutes.

# Thumbprint Cookies

- 1/2 C butter, softened
- 1/3 C sugar
- 2 eggs
- 1/2 tsp salt
- 1/4 tsp baking powder
- 1/4 tsp baking soda
- 1/2 tsp vanilla
- Jelly

ROOT INGREDIENTS

- 1/3 C gluten free All purpose flour
- 1 C regular All purpose flour

*If only making 1 recipe of regular or gluten free cookies, use 1 1/2 Cups of either flour.*

Mix the first 7 ingredients together. Separate mixture, take 1/2 C mixture put it in a separate bowl (this will be your gluten free mix). Add 1/3 C gluten free flour and mix. In the first bowl add 1 C regular flour and mix. Take pieces of dough and roll dough into 1 inch size ball. Push your thumb down in the middle of ball. Add 1 tsp of jelly-I used jelly. Bake at 375 for 10 minutes.

# Sugar Cookies

- 3/4 C sugar
- 1/2 tbsp butter, melted
- 1 egg
- 1 tsp vanilla
- 3/4 C baking powder
- 1/4 tsp salt

ICING

- 1 C powdered sugar
- 1 egg white
- 1 tsp vanilla
- 1 tbsp milk (I used original unsweetened almond milk)
- Food coloring (optional)

ROOT INGREDIENTS

- 1/2 C + 1 tbsp gluten free All purpose flour
- 1 1/3 C regular All purpose flour

*If only making 1 recipe of regular or gluten free cookies, use 1 1/2 Cups of either flour.*

Mix first 3 ingredients then mix in baking powder and salt. Separate mixture, take 1/3 C mixture put it in a separate bowl (this will be your gluten free mix). Add 1/2 C + 1 tbsp gluten free flour and 1/4 tsp xanthan gum and mix. In the first bowl add 1 1/3 C regular flour and mix. When I put the flour in the mix I mix it with my hands. Do the gluten free dough first. Roll out the dough to 1/4 inch thickness. I used a cup to cut out the cookies. Put on sprayed cookie sheet. Bake at 350 for 7-8 minutes, until golden color on bottom.

Allow cookies to cool for 1 hour before frosting them.

DESSERT | 73

# Coconut Macaroons

*I had always wanted to make these but didn't know how. My friend Jess is a chef and she came over one day and showed me. Easy and yummy!*

- 3 egg whites
- 3/4 C sugar
- 2 pinches of salt
- 1 tsp vanilla
- 14 oz coconut

Using a blender, whip up the egg whites and sugar until stiff peaks happen-approximately 8 minutes. Around 7 minutes in add salt and vanilla. Using a plastic spatula, gently mix in the coconut. Don't overmix as it will deflate the egg whites. Put the bowl in the refrigerator for 20 minutes. Cover 2 cookie sheets with parchment paper. After 20 minutes, take mixture out and using a large tablespoon, drop the macaroon mixture onto the parchment paper. Bake at 350 for 15 minutes.

# Grimace

*My memere used to make these when my father was young. My mother learned how to make them. It's a dry cookie that goes great with coffee or tea.*

- 1 C brown sugar
- 4 oz shortening
- 1 egg
- 1/4 C water
- 1 tsp baking powder

### ROOT INGREDIENTS

- 1 1/4 C gluten free All purpose flour
- 1 1/4 C regular All purpose flour

*\*If only making 1 recipe of regular or gluten free cookies, use 2 1/2 Cups of either flour.*

Mix water, 2 oz shortening, egg and baking powder together. Separate the dough in half and put it in a separate bowl (this will be your gluten free mix). Add 1 1/4 C gluten free flour and 1/4 tsp xanthan gum and mix. In the first bowl add 1 1/4 C regular flour and mix. Roll out the gluten free dough as thin as possible. Spread 1 oz of shortening on the dough. Spread 1/2 C of brown sugar on the shortening and roll up the dough. Do the same process for the regular dough recipe. Slice both doughs and put on greased cookie sheets. Bake in the oven at 350 for 15 minutes.

# Potpouri

*Appetizers, party favorites or just a snack*

# Chicken Gravy

- 3 C chicken broth, gluten free
- 1/2 tsp salt
- 1/2 tsp pepper
- 1/2 tsp garlic powder
- 2 tbsp corn starch
- 4 oz water

In a pot, bring chicken broth to a boil. Add salt, pepper and garlic powder. In a cup add cornstarch and water and mix. To the boiling broth stir in the cornstarch mixture. Let boil 1 minute and it is done.

# Coleslaw

- 1 medium red cabbage, shredded
- 1 medium green cabbage, shredded
- 2 large carrots, shredded
- 1/2 C mayonnaise
- 2 tbsp sugar
- 1 1/2 tbsp lemon juice
- 1 tbsp vinegar
- 1/2 tsp pepper
- 1/4 tsp salt

Add the cabbage and carrots in a bowl and toss to mix. In a separate bowl, stir the mayonnaise, sugar, lemon juice, vinegar, salt, and pepper together. Pour the mixture over the coleslaw mix and mix with a large spoon. Cover and put in refrigerator for 1 hour, then serve.

# Honey Dijon Salad Dressing

- 1/4 C + 1 tbsp Dijon mustard
- 1/4 C honey
- 1/4 C apple cider vinegar
- 1 tsp salt
- 1/3 C olive oil

In a bowl whisk together all the ingredients until creamy. Can store in refrigerator for up to 3 days.

# Belly Burn Salad Dressing

- 1/2 C apple cider vinegar
- 1/4 C olive oil
- 2 tbsp lemon juice
- 4 small cloves garlic, minced
- Pinch of salt
- Pinch of pepper

In a bowl whisk all the ingredients together. Can store in refrigerator for up to 3 days.

# Italian Salad Dressing

- 1/2 tsp onion powder
- 1 tsp sugar
- 1 tsp oregano
- 1/4 tsp pepper
- 1/8 tsp thyme
- 1/4 tsp basil
- 1/4 tsp parsley
- 1/8 tsp garlic powder
- 1/2 tsp salt
- 1/4 C vinegar, gluten free
- 1/3 C olive oil

Add the first 9 ingredients in a bowl and mix together. Add vinegar and olive oil and whisk until completely mixed together.

# DRINKS

*A lot of alcohols have gluten in them. I personally like wine, which is naturally GF. Please read the Alcohol section of the book to find what is gluten free. Here is a shortcut when making drinks. An average shot glass is 2 oz or 4 tbsp.*

# Tropical Passion

- 6 shots gluten free vodka
- 2 liters ginger ale
- 24 oz pineapple juice
- Slices of 1 orange
- Small jar of maraschino cherries

Add all the ingredients together, stir and enjoy!

# Vodka Cranberry Cocktail

- 8 oz cranberry juice
- 3 oz orange juice
- 1/4 C cranberries
- 1/4 C simple syrup
- 1/4 C vodka, gluten free
- Juice of 1 lime
- 8 oz seltzer

Combine the first 6 ingredients in a cocktail shaker. Add ice, cover and shake until chilled. Add seltzer to shaker and pour in glass.

# Party Punch

*This punch is a family party favorite! You have the option of serving it with or without alcohol.*

- 2 liters ginger ale
- 1 can frozen lemonade w/ water
- 1 can frozen pineapple juice w/water
- 1/2 gallon orange sherbet (I used 8 oz orange juice)
- 1 jar maraschino cherries with juice
- 1 C vodka, gluten free

Add all the ingredients together in a large punch bowl. The frozen cherries will keep it cold.

# Cocoa Mo

- 8 oz ice
- 3 tbsp coffee syrup
- 8 oz milk (I used original unsweetened almond milk)
- 2 oz vodka, gluten free
- 1/4 tsp cocoa, unsweetened

Put the first 4 ingredients in a blender on high for 1 minute. Pour in a glass and add the cocoa on top.

# Blueberry Mojito

To make a simple syrup: Add 1 C water and 1 C sugar in a pot and bring to a boil. Lower to a simmer and stir until sugar is melted. Store in the refrigerator for 4 weeks.

- 10 large mint leaves
- 1/2 C blueberries
- 2 oz simple syrup
- 2 tsp lime, juiced
- 2 oz rum, gluten free
- 1/2 C club soda

In a cocktail shaker, Add the blueberries, mint and simple syrup. Use the end of a wooden spoon or cocktail muddler to muddle the blueberries and mint. Add the rum, lime juice, and some ice to the shaker and shake vigorously. Add ice cubes to your glass, fill your glass and add the club soda and stir gently. Garnish with a lime wedge and a few blueberries to serve.

MY FIRST COOKBOOK PUBLISHED IN 2017

# GLUTEN AND GLUTEN FREE COOKING IN PERFECT HARMONY

The One Recipe Solution to Accommodate Everyone

## Lucie Cote Contente

www.glutenandglutenfreecookinginperfectharmony.com

CPSIA information can be obtained
at www.ICGtesting.com
Printed in the USA
FSHW010005310119
55374FS